The book of
Irish Songs
yer oul' fella always sang
when he was jarred at
a hooley

The Feckin' Collection

Your eyes they shine like diamonds

The book of Irish Songs yer oul' fella always sang when he was jarred at a hooley

Colin Murphy & Donal O'Dea

THE O'BRIEN PRESS
DUBLIN

First published 2004 by The O'Brien Press Ltd,
20 Victoria Road, Dublin 6, Ireland.
Tel: +353 1 4923333; Fax: +353 1 4922777
E-mail: books@obrien.ie
Website: www.obrien.ie
Reprinted 2004.

ISBN: 0-86278-828-5

British Library Cataloguing-in-Publication Data
Murphy, Colin
The book of Irish songs yer oul' fella always sang when he was jarred at
a hooley. - (Feckin' collection ; bk. 1)
1.Songs, Irish - Texts
2.Ballads, Irish - Texts
I.Title II.O'Dea, Donal
782.4'20268

2 3 4 5 6 7 8 9 10
04 05 06 07 08

Printing: Oriental Press, Dubai

CONTENTS

The Banks of My Own Lovely Lee

John Fitzgerald

The Cork National Anthem, as it is also known, is just one in a long line of ballads in which an exile laments the loss of his homeland. There he is in America, loaded with spondulicks, dreaming of all he's left behind: freezing cold, no plumbing, no food. And he wants to come back? Were they all feckin' nuts?

How oft do my thoughts in their fancy take flight
To the home of my childhood away,
To the days when each patriot's vision seemed bright
Ere I dreamed that those joys should decay.
When my heart was as light as the wild winds that blow
Down the Mardyke through each elm tree,
Where I sported and played 'neath each green
leafy shade
On the banks of my own lovely Lee.
*Where I sported and played 'neath each green leafy
shade, on the banks of my own lovely Lee.*

And then in the springtime of laughter and song
Can I ever forget the sweet hours?
With the friends of my youth as we rambled along
'Mongst the green mossy banks and wild flowers.
Then when the evening sun sinking to rest
Sheds its golden light over the sea
The maid with her lover the wild daisies pressed
On the banks of my own lovely Lee.
The maid with her lover ...

'Tis a beautiful land this dear isle of song
Its gems shed their light to the world
And her faithful sons bore thro' ages of wrong,
The standard St Patrick unfurled.
Oh would I were there with the friends I love best
And my fond bosom's partner with me,
We'd roam thy banks over, and when weary we'd rest
By thy waters, my own lovely Lee.
We'd roam thy banks over ...

Oh what joys should be mine ere this life should
decline
To seek shells on thy sea-girdled shore.
While the steel-feathered eagle, oft splashing the
brine
Brings longing for freedom once more.
Oh all that on earth I wish for or crave
Is that my last crimson drop be for thee,
To moisten the grass of my forefathers' grave
On the banks of my own lovely Lee.
To moisten the grass of my forefathers' grave
On the banks of my own lovely Lee.

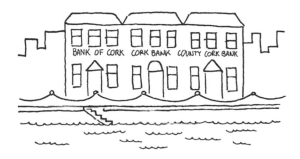

The Black Velvet Band

Traditional

A cautionary tale for you young bucks that get all gooey-eyed at the sight of a pretty face and a fine pair of hips. Beware! She's the devil in disguise, bent on leading you astray and whisking you off to Van Dieman's Land for seven years. Or nowadays to the Costa del Sol for fourteen days, which, when you think of it, is probably worse.

In a neat little town they call Belfast,
Apprenticed to trade I was bound,
And many's the hour of sweet happiness,
I spent in that neat little town,
Till a strange misfortune overtook me,
Which caused me to stray from the land,
Far away from my friends and relations,
Betrayed by the black velvet band.

Chorus:

Her eyes they shone like diamonds,
You'd think her the queen of the land,
And her hair hung over her shoulder,
Tied up with a black velvet band.

I SENTENCE YOU TO TWO
WEEKS IN LANZAROTE

As I went walking down Broadway,
Not intending to stay very long,
Who should I see but a fine colleen,
As she came a-traipsing along.
A watch she pulled out of her pocket,
And slipped it right into my hand,
On the very first day that I met her,
Bad luck to the black velvet band.

Chorus

Before the judge and the jury,
Next morning we both did appear,
And the gentleman swore to the jury,
The case was proven quite clear.
For seven years transportation,
Down to the Van Dieman's Land,
Far away from my friends and relations,
To follow her black velvet band.

Chorus

Oh all you brave young fellows,
A warning now take you from me,
Beware of the pretty young damsels,
You might meet around in Tralee.
They'll treat you to whiskey and porter,
Until you're unable to stand,
And before you have time for to leave them,
You'll be sent down to Van Dieman's Land.

Bunch of Thyme

Traditional

This might seem an odd one, but thyme in this instance appears to be a metaphor for virginity. Or one could say that in more innocent days it was a metaphor for innocence. Then again, it could be a metaphor for youth. Or for time. Or maybe the whole thing is just a recipe for vegetable bleedin' soup.

Come all ye maidens young and fair,
All you that are blooming in your prime.
Always beware and keep your garden fair,
Let no man steal away your thyme.

Chorus:

For thyme it is a precious thing,
And thyme brings all things to my mind.
Thyme with all its flavours, along with all its joys,
Thyme brings all things to my mind.

Once I had a bunch of thyme,
I thought it never would decay.
Then came a lusty sailor,

who chanced to pass my way,
and stole my bunch of thyme away.

Chorus

The sailor gave to me a rose,
A rose that never would decay.
He gave it to me to keep me reminded
Of when he stole my thyme away.

Chorus

VERY TASTY. I WOULDN'T MIND
SOME OF THAT!!!

The Cliffs of Dooneen

Traditional

This one is a big favourite at sing-songs, thanks mainly to the fact that a well-known Irish folk band popularised it in the Seventies. However, most drunken party-goers usually only get about as far as 'Watching all the wild flowers la da da di da...' or thereabouts. They then quickly descend into 'Na na lan di da. Da di da na di da da la ... the Cliffs of Dooneen.'

You may travel far far from your own native home;
Far away o'er the mountains, far away o'er
the foam,
But of all the fine places that I've ever been
Sure there's none can compare with the cliffs
of Dooneen.

Take a view o'er the mountains, fine sights
you'll see there,
You'll see the high rocky mountains o'er the
west coast of Clare;
Oh the towns of Kilkee and Kilrush can be seen
From the high rocky slopes round the cliffs
of Dooneen.

It's a nice place to be on a fine summer's day
Watching all the wild flowers that ne'er do decay,
Oh the hares and lofty pheasants are plain to
be seen,
Making homes for their young round the cliffs
of Dooneen.

Fare thee well to Doneen, fare thee well for a while,
And to all the kind people I'm leaving behind;
To the streams and the meadows where late
I have been
And the high rocky slopes round the cliffs
of Dooneen.

AH THE CLIFFS OF DOO...HIC....NEEN...

Danny Boy

Fred Weatherly

*When me Auntie Maureen used to sing this –
Ireland's favourite song of love and death – it
never failed to bring a tear to me eye. I
swear, her voice really was that bad.*

Oh Danny boy, the pipes, the pipes are calling
From glen to glen, and down the mountain side.
The summer's gone, and all the flowers
are dying
'Tis you, 'tis you must go and I must bide.

But come you back when summer's in the meadow,
Or when the valley's hushed and white with snow,
'Tis I'll be here in sunshine or in shadow,
Oh Danny boy, oh Danny boy, I love you so.

And if you come, when all the flowers are dying,
And I am dead, as dead I well may be,
You'll come and find the place where I am lying,
And kneel and say an 'Ave' there for me.

And I shall hear, though soft you tread above me,
And all my dreams will warmer, sweeter be.
And you will kneel and tell me that you love me
And I shall sleep in peace until you come to me.

SOMEONE SHUT HER UP. I CAN'T
TAKE MUCH MORE OF THIS!

Galway Bay

Francis A Fahey

In the final verse, the singer exhorts God to grant him his personal heaven by returning him home to his beloved Galway. Fair enough. But if such a system is actually in operation, I wonder, God, could I have Bermuda?

It's far away I am today
From scenes I roamed a boy,
And long ago the hour, I know
I first saw Illinois.
But time nor tide, not waters wide,
Can wean my heart away,
For ever true it flies to you
My own dear Galway Bay.

A prouder man I'd walk the land
In health and peace of mind,
If I might toil and strive and moil,
Nor cast one thought behind;
But what would be the world to me,
Its rank and rich array,
If memory I lost of thee,
My poor old Galway Bay.

Oh, grey and bleak, by shore and creek,
The rugged rocks abound,
But sweeter green the grass between
Than grows on Irish ground.
So friendship fond, all wealth beyond,
And love that lives alway,
Bless each poor home beside your foam,
My dear old Galway Bay.

Had I youth's blood and hopeful mood
And heart of fire once more,
For all the gold the earth might hold,
I'd never quit your shore;
I'd live content whate'er God sent,
With neighbours old and grey,
And lay my bones 'neath churchyard stones,
Beside you, Galway Bay.

The blessing of a poor old man
Be with you night and day,
The blessings of a lonely man
Whose heart will soon be clay.
'Tis all the Heaven I'd ask of God
Upon my dying day,
My soul to soar for evermore
Above you, Galway Bay.

The Holy Ground

Traditional

The basic story is this: Man leaves girl to go to sea, promising to return. Storm hits ship. Ship survives. Man goes to pub, gets locked. Man returns to sea. Forgets about girl. Typical Irish male.

Fare thee well, my lovely Dinah, a thousand
times adieu.
We are bound away from the Holy Ground and
the girls we love so true.
We'll sail the salt seas over and we'll return
for sure,
To see again the girls we love and the Holy
Ground once more.

Chorus:

(Yelled) Fine girl you are!
(Sung) You're the girl that I adore,
And still I live in hope to see the Holy Ground
once more.
(Yelled) Fine girl you are!

Now when we're out a-sailing and you are
far behind,
Fine letters will I write to you with the secrets
of my mind.

The secrets of my mind, my girl, you're the girl
that I adore,
And still I live in hope to see the Holy Ground
once more.

Chorus

Oh now the storm is raging and we are far from
shore,
The poor old ship she's sinking fast and the rigging
is all tore.
The night is dark and dreary, we can scarcely see
the moon,
But still I live in hope to see the Holy Ground
once more.

Chorus

And now the storm is over and we are safe
on shore,
We'll drink a toast to the Holy Ground and the
girls that we adore.
We'll drink strong ale and porter and we'll make
the rafters roar,
And when our money is all spent we'll go to sea
once more.

Chorus

I'll Take You Home Again, Kathleen

Thomas Westendorf

*Ah, what a great old traditional Irish song!
Except that it's not Irish at all. It was written
by a German called Westendorf while he was
living in Illinois. Kathleen, his missus, was
always whingeing about going back to the old
sod (Ireland that is, not Westendorf), so he
wrote this for her, to shut her up.*

I'll take you home again, Kathleen,
Across the ocean wild and wide.
To where your heart has ever been,
Since first you were my bonnie bride.
The roses all have left your cheek,
I've watched them fade away and die;
Your voice is sad when e'er you speak
And tears bedim your loving eyes.

Chorus:

Oh, I will take you back, Kathleen,
To where your heart will feel no pain,
And when the fields are fresh and green
I'll take you to your home again.

I know you love me, Kathleen, dear,
Your heart was ever fond and true.
I always feel when you are near
That life holds nothing dear but you.
The smiles that once you gave to me
I scarcely ever see them now,
Though many, many times I see
A dark'ning shadow on your brow.

Chorus

To that dear home beyond the sea,
My Kathleen shall again return.
And when thy old friends welcome thee,
Thy loving heart will cease to yearn.
Where laughs the little silver stream,
Beside your mother's humble cot,
And brightest rays of sunshine gleam,
There all your grief will be forgot.

Chorus

WOULD YOU C'MON KATHLEEN, IT'S WAY PAST CLOSING TIME!

I'll Tell Me Ma

Traditional

Next time you're singing away happily to this one, take pause for a moment during the song to ask yourself one simple question: 'How the hell can anyone wear bells on their toes?' Must be a Belfast thing.

I'll tell me ma, when I go home,
The boys won't leave the girls alone,
They pulled my hair and stole my comb,
And that's alright till I go home.

Chorus:

She is handsome, she is pretty,
She is the belle of Belfast city.
She is courtin', one, two, three.
Please, won't you tell me who is she?

GET YOUR TOE BELLS , TWO
FOR A POUND. TOE BELLS
TWO FOR A POUND!!!

Chorus

Albert Mooney says he loves her,
All the boys are fighting for her.
They rap at the door and ring at the bell,
Saying 'Oh my true love, are you well?'
Out she comes as white as snow,
Rings on her fingers, bells on her toes,
Old Johnny Murray says she'll die,
If she doesn't get the fellow with the roving eye.

Chorus

Let the wind and the rain and the hail blow high,
And the snow come tumblin' from the sky,
She's as sweet as apple pie,
And she'll get her own lad by and by.
When she gets a lad of her own,
She won't tell her ma when she comes home,
Let them all come as they will,
But it's Albert Mooney she loves still.

Chorus

The Irish Rover

Traditional

This is one of those tunes that when your Da or your uncle starts crowing it at the hooley after the wedding, it seems to last forever, or at least as long as it took the Irish Rover to wander the high seas. And all the while you're left standing there, stupid false grin on your gob, pretending to tap your foot to the tune and dying to go to the bar for a pint. So remember, as soon as it stops, it's time to abandon ship.

In the year of our Lord, eighteen hundred and six
We set sail from the fair cove of Cork.
We were bound far away with a cargo of bricks
For the fine city hall of New York.
In a very fine craft, she was rigged fore and aft
And oh, how the wild winds drove her.
She had twenty-three masts and withstood
many a blast
And we called her the Irish Rover.

There was Barney McGee from the banks of the Lee,
There was Hogan from County Tyrone.
There was Johnny McGurk who was scared stiff
of work
And a chap from Westmeath called Malone.
There was Slugger O'Toole who was drunk as a rule,

And fighting Bill Casey from Dover.
There was Dooley from Clare who was strong as a
bear,
And was skipper of the Irish Rover.

We had one million bales of old billy goats' tails,
We had two million buckets of stones.
We had three million sides of old blind horses hides,
We had four million packets of bones.
We had five million hogs, we had six million dogs,
And seven million barrels of porter.
We had eight million bags of the best Sligo rags
In the hold of the Irish Rover.

We had sailed seven years when the measles broke
out
And the ship lost her way in a fog.
And the whole of the crew was reduced unto two,
'Twas myself and the captain's old dog.
Then the ship struck a rock. Oh Lord, what a shock,
And then she heeled right over,
Turned nine times around, and the poor dog was
drowned,
I'm the last of the Irish Rover.

25

Lanigan's Ball

Neil Bryant/Tony Pastor

Besides the usual content of death; war, tragedy, butchered innocents, famine, etc, occasionally we Irish found room for a laugh in our musical hearts. But don't get too used to it, we'll be back to the blood and the broken hearts before you know it. In fact, normal service will resume just as soon as Lanigan has held his rather lengthy ball.

In the town of Athy one Jeremy Lanigan,
Battered away 'til he hadn't a pound.
His father he died and made him a man again,
Left him a farm and ten acres of ground.
He gave a grand party to friends and relations
Who didn't forget him when sent to the wall,
And if you'll but listen I'll make your eyes glisten
Of the rows and the ructions of Lanigan's Ball.

Chorus:

Six long months I spent in Dublin,
Six long months doing nothing at all.
Six long months I spent in Dublin,
Learning to dance for Lanigan's ball.

Myself to be sure got free invitations,
For all the nice girls and boys I might ask,
And just in a minute both friends and relations
Were dancing as merry as bees 'round a cask.
Judy O'Daly, that nice little milliner,
She tipped me a wink for to give her a call,
And I soon arrived with Timothy Galligan
Just in good time for Lanigan's Ball.

Chorus

There were lashings of punch and wine
for the ladies,
Potatoes and cakes; there was bacon and tea.
There were the Nolans, Dolans, O'Gradys
Courting the girls and dancing away.
Songs they went 'round as plenty as water,
'The harp that once sounded in Tara's old hall,'
'Sweet Nelly Gray' and 'The Rat Catcher's
Daughter,'
All singing together at Lanigan's Ball.

Chorus

They were doing all kinds of nonsensical polkas
All 'round the room in a great whirly-gig.
Julia and I, we banished their nonsense
And tipped them the twist of a reel and a jig.
And oh how the girls they got all mad at me
Danced 'til you'd think the ceiling would fall.
For I spent three weeks at Brooks' Academy
Learning new steps for Lanigan's Ball.

Chorus

Boys were all merry and the girls they were hearty,
And danced all around in couples and groups.
'Til an accident happened, young Terence
McCarthy,
He put his right leg throug Miss Finnerty's hoops.
The poor creature fainted and cried, 'Meelia murther,'
Called for her brothers and gathered them all.
Carmody swore that he'd go no further
'Til he'd had satisfaction at Lanigan's Ball.

Chorus

In the midst of the row Miss Kerrigan fainted,
Her cheeks at the same time as red as a rose.
Some of the lads declared she was painted,
She took a small drop too much, I suppose.

Her sweetheart, Ned Morgan, so powerful
and able,
When he saw his fair colleen stretched out by
the wall,
He tore the left leg from under the table
And smashed all the dishes at Lanigan's Ball.

Chorus

Boys, oh boys, 'twas then there were runctions.
Myself got a lick from big Phelim McHugh.
But I soon replied to his kind introduction
And kicked up a terrible hullabaloo.
Old Casey, the piper, was near being strangled,
They squeezed up his pipes, bellows, chanters
and all.
The girls in their ribbons, they got all entangled,
And that put an end to Lanigan's Ball.

Leaving of Liverpool

Traditional

OK, strictly speaking this isn't Irish. Come to think of it, loosely speaking it isn't Irish either. But it does crop up regularly at Irish sing-songs and it does have all the basic ingredients. It's akin to one of those Brits we've adopted as one of our own – like St Patrick. And we'll allow it the great privilege of being Irish for as long as we can get something out of it for nothing.

Farewell to Prince's Landing Stage,
River Mersey, fare thee well.
I am bound for California,
A place I know right well.

Chorus:

So fare thee well, my own true love,
When I return united we will be.
It's not the leaving of Liverpool that's grieving me
But my darling when I think of thee.

I'm bound off for California
By the way of stormy Cape Horn.
And I'm bound to write you a letter, love,
When I am homeward bound.

Chorus

I have signed on a Yankee Clipper ship,
Davy Crockett is her name.
And Burgess is the captain of her,
And they say she's a floating hell.
Chorus

I have shipped with Burgess once before,
And I think I know him well.
If a man's a seaman, he can get along,
If not, then he's sure in hell.

Chorus

Farewell to lower Frederick Street,
Ensign Terrace and Park Lane.
For I think it will be a long, long time
Before I see you again.

Chorus

Oh the sun is on the harbour, love,
And I wish I could remain,
For I know it will be a long, long time
Before I see you again.

LIVERPOOL 0: WYCOMBE 3
THAT'S IT. I'M LEAVING.

Maids When You're Young Never Wed an Old Man

Traditional

The filthiest, most suggestive, rudest and most downright offensive song you're ever likely to hear sung at an Irish social function. Now, bet you're dying to read the lyrics!

An old man came courting me, hey ding doorum-da,
An old man came courting me, me being young,
An old man came courting me, saying 'would
you marry me',
Maids when you're young, never wed an old man.

Chorus:
For he's got no faloo-doo-rum,
Fal-diddle-oo-doo-rum,
He's got no faloo-doo-rum, Fa-diddle-day,
He's got no faloo-doo-rum,
Lost his ding-doo-reeum,
Maids when you're young, never wed an old man.

When this old man comes to bed, hey ding
doorum-da,
When this old man comes to bed, me being young,
When this old man comes to bed, he lays like he
was dead,
Maids when you're young, never wed an old man.

Chorus

When this old man goes to sleep, hey ding
doorum-da,
When this old man goes to sleep, me being young,
When this old man goes to sleep, out of bed
I do creep,
Into the arms of a handsome young man.

Chorus

I wish this old man would die, hey ding
doorum-da,
I wish this old man would die, me being young,
I wish this old man would die, I'd make the
money fly,
Girls for your sake, never wed an old man.

Chorus

A young man is my delight, hey ding doorum-da,
A young man is my delight, me being young,
A young man is my delight, he'll kiss you
day and night,
Maids when you're young,
never wed an old man.

I THINK I'VE
FOUND THE
PROBLEM MR
KELLY. IT
WOULD
APPEAR YOU
HAVE NO
'FALOO DOO
RUM'.

The Minstrel Boy

Thomas Moore

A sad tale of Ireland's national emblem, the harp, which is a totally appropriate symbol for modern Ireland, because for the last eighty years the entire country has been run by pulling strings.

The minstrel boy to the war is gone
In the ranks of death you will find him.
His father's sword he has girded on
And his wild harp slung behind him.

'Land of Song!' said the warrior bard
'Though all the world betray thee,
One sword, at least, thy rights shall guard,
One faithful harp shall praise thee!'

The minstrel fell! But the foeman's steel
Could not bring that proud soul under.
The harp he loved ne'er spoke again
For he tore its chords asunder.

And said, 'No chains shall sully thee
Thou soul of love and bravery!
Thy songs were made for the pure and free,
They shall never sound in slavery!'

YOU PLUCK MY HARP AND I'LL
PLUCK YOURS

Cockles and Mussels (Molly Malone)

James Yorkston

The famous ditty about Molly Malone – or as she's known to Dubs since they erected a rather well-endowed statue in her honour – 'The Tart with the Cart' or the slightly more complimentary 'Dish with the Fish'.

In Dublin's fair city where the girls are so pretty
I first set my eyes on sweet Molly Malone,
As she wheeled her wheelbarrow
Through streets broad and narrow,
Crying, 'Cockles and mussels, alive, alive–o!'

Chorus:

Alive, alive-o, alive, alive-o,
Crying, 'Cockles and mussels, alive, alive–o!'

She was a fishmonger and sure 'twas no wonder,
For so were her mother and father before;
And they each wheeled their barrow
Through streets broad and narrow,
Crying, 'Cockles and mussels, alive, alive–o!'

Chorus

She died of a fever and no one could save her,
And that was the end of sweet Molly Malone.
But her ghost wheels her barrow
Through streets broad and narrow,
Crying, 'Cockles and mussels, alive, alive–o!'

Chorus

COCKLES AND MUSSELS AND
TICKETS TO THE HOGAN STAND,
ALIVE ALIVE–O!!!

The Mountains of Mourne

Percy French

Irish society at the time was shocked by the notion of topless women wandering the streets of London as referred to in verse two. And of course it's a complete coincidence that in the months following the release of the song, emigration of Irish males to London rose by approximately one thousand per cent!

Oh Mary, this London's a wonderful sight
With people here workin' by day and by night.
They don't sow potatoes, nor barley, nor wheat,
But there's gangs of them diggin' for gold in
the street.
At least when I asked them that's what I was told,
So I just took a hand at this diggin' for gold,
But for all that I found there I might as well be,
Where the mountains of Mourne sweep down
to the sea.

I believe that when writin' a wish you expressed
As to how the fine ladies in London were dressed.
Well if you'll believe me, when asked to a ball,
Faith, they don't wear no top to their dresses at all.
I've seen them myself and you could not in truth
Say if they were bound for a ball or a bath.
Don't be startin' them fashions now, Mary MacCree,

Where the mountains of Mourne sweep down
to the sea.

You remember young Peter O'Loughlin of course.
Well now he is here at the head of the Force.
I met him today, I was crossing the Strand,
And he stopped the whole street with a wave
of his hand.
And there we stood talking of days that are gone
While the whole population of London looked on;
But for all these great powers, he's wishful, like me
To be back where the dark Mourne sweeps down
to the sea.

There's beautiful girls here, oh never you mind,
With beautiful shapes Nature never designed.
And lovely complexions, all roses and cream,
But let me remark with regard to the same,
That if that those roses you venture to sip,
The colours might all come away on your lip.
So I'll wait for the wild rose that's waitin' for me
In the place where the dark Mourne sweeps down
to the sea.

WHY DO I KEEP
THINKING OF
THE MOUNTAINS
OF MOURNE?

A Nation Once Again

Thomas Davis

Ah, this rousing ballad stirs up many a memory of childhood for Irishmen everywhere. The bleeding thing was battered into you in school by the fanatically republican Christian Brothers and when you hear it nowadays it certainly makes you want to rise up, grab them by their clerical collars and beat the living bejaysus out of them.

When boyhood's fire was in my blood
I read of ancient freemen,
For Greece and Rome who bravely stood,
Three hundred men and three men;
And then I prayed I yet might see
Our fetters rent in twain,
And Ireland, long a province, be
A nation once again!

Chorus:

A nation once again,
A nation once again,
And Ireland, long a province, be
A nation once again!

And from that time, through wildest woe,
That hope has shone a far light,

Nor could love's brightest summer glow
Outshine that solemn starlight;
It seemed to watch above my head
In forum, field and fane,
Its angel voice sang round my bed,
A nation once again!

Chorus

It whispered, too, that freedom's ark
And service high and holy,
Would be profaned by feelings dark
And passions vain or lowly;
For freedom comes from God's right hand,
And needs a Godly train;
And righteous men must make our land
A nation once again!

Chorus

So as I grew from boy to man,
I bent me to that bidding,
My spirit of each selfish plan
And cruel passion ridding;
For thus I hoped some day to aid,
Oh, can such hope be vain?
When my dear country shall be
A nation once again!
Chorus

SING IT, YE
LITTLE FECKERS!!
A NATION ONCE
AGAIN!! ... A
NATION ONCE
AGAIN !!...

Old Maid in the Garret

A pity we can't introduce the oul' one in this little ditty to some of the lonely male hearts who populate so many other Irish ballads. Because this babe is positively gagging for it.

I have often heard it said from my father and my
mother,
That going to a weddin' is the makings of another.
And if this be so then I'll go without a biddin',
Oh it's kind providence won't you send me to
a weddin'.

Chorus:

And it's oh dear me! How will it be,
If I die an old maid in the garret?

Now there's my sister Jean, she's not handsome or
goodlookin',
Scarcely sixteen, and a fella she was courtin'.
Now she's twenty-four, with a son and a daughter,
Here am I at forty-five and I've never had an offer!

Chorus

MUST FIND MAN ... MUST

I can cook and I can sew, I can keep the house right tidy,
Rise up in the morning and get the breakfast ready.
But there's nothing in this wide world would make me so cheery
As a wee fat man who would call me his own dearie!

Chorus

So come landsman, come townsman, come tinker or come tailor,
Come fiddler or come dancer, come ploughman or come sailor.
Come rich man, come poor man, come fool or come witty,
Come any man at all who would marry me for pity.

Chorus

Oh well I'm away home, for there's nobody heedin',
There's nobody heedin' to poor Annie's pleadin'.
And I'm away home to me own wee-bit garret,
If I can't get a man, then I'll surely get a parrot.

Chorus

FIND MAN ... MUST FIND MAN

43

Raggle Taggle Gypsy

Traditional

This is the one where everyone knows the tune, but only one die-hard knows all the lyrics and everyone else joins in irritatingly on the last three words of each verse.

There were three gypsies a-come to my door,
And downstairs ran this lady, O!
One sang high and another sang low,
And the other sang bonny, bonny, Biscayo!

Then she pulled off her silk finished gown
And put on hose of leather, O!
The ragged ragged rags about our door,
She's gone with the raggle taggle gypsy, O!

It was late last night when my lord came home,
Enquiring for his lady, O!
The servants said, on every hand,
She's gone with the raggle taggle gypsy, O!

Oh, saddle me my milk-white steed,
Go and fetch me my pony, O!
That I may ride and seek my bride,
Who is gone with the raggle taggle gypsy, O!

Oh, he rode high and he rode low,
He rode through the wood and copses, O,
Until he came to an open field,
And there he espied his lady, O!

What makes you leave your house and land?
What makes you leave your money, O?
What makes you leave your new wedded lord
To go with the raggle taggle gypsy, O?

What care I for my house and my land?
What care I for my money, O?
What care I for my new wedded lord?
I'm off with the raggle taggle gypsy, O!

Last night you slept on a goose-feather bed,
With the sheet turned down so bravely, O!
And tonight you'll sleep in a cold open field,
Along with the raggle taggle gypsy, O!

What care I for a goose-feather bed?
With the sheet turned down so bravely, O!
For tonight I shall sleep in a cold open field,
Along with the raggle taggle gypsy, O!

BLAH BLAH DI BLAH, BLAH DI BLAH DI BLAH.
RAGGLE TAGGLE TO DE RAGGLE TAGGLE GYPSY O!

The Rocky Road to Dublin

Traditional

Down the years there have been many inter-pretations (and versions) of the final, emotive cry which concludes each verse – 'Whack follol de rah!' Some say its etymology lies deep in Irish pre-history, others that it's a corruption of an old Celtic war cry and others still believe that the man who penned it was simply pissed as a newt.

In the merry month of June, when first from home I started,
And left the girls alone, sad and broken-hearted.
Shook hands with father dear, kissed my darling mother,
Drank a pint of beer, my grief and tears to smother;
Then off to reap the corn, and leave where I was born,
I cut a stout blackthorn to banish ghost and goblin;
With a pair of brand new brogues I rattled o'er the bogs,
Sure I frightened all the dogs on the rocky road to Dublin.

Chorus:

One, two, three, four, five,
Hunt the hare and turn her down the rocky road
And all the way to Dublin, whack follol de rah!

In Mullingar that night I rested limbs so weary,
Started by daylight with spirits light and airy;
Took a drop of the pure to keep me heart from sinking,
That's always an Irishman's cure whene'er he's
on for drinking,
To see the lassies smile, laughing all the while
At my comical style, set my heart a-bubblin';
They asked if I was hired, the wages I required,
Until I was almost tired of the rocky road to Dublin.

Chorus

In Dublin next arrived, I thought It was a pity
To be soon deprived of a view of that fine city;
'Twas then I took a stroll all among the quality,
My bundle then was stole in a neat locality.
Something crossed my mind, thinks I, I'll look behind,
No bundle could I find upon my stick a-wobblin;
Inquiring for the rogue, they said my Connaught brogue,
Wasn't much in vogue on the rocky road to Dublin.

A coachman raised his hand as if myself was wantin',
I went up to a stand full of cars for jauntin'.
Step up, my boy! says he; ah! that I will with
pleasure,
And to the Strawberry Beds I'll drive you at your
leisure,
A strawberry bed, says I. Faith! that would be too
high,
On one of straw I'll lie, and the berries won't
be troublin'.
He drove me out so far, upon an outside car.
Faith! such a jolting never were, on the rocky road
to Dublin.

Chorus

I soon got out of that, my spirits never failing,
I landed on the quay just as the ship was sailing.
The captain at me roared, swore that no room had
he,
But when I leapt on board, a cabin found for
Paddy.
Down among the pigs I played with rummy rigs,
Danced some hearty jigs, with the water round me
bubblin'.
But when off Holyhead I wished that I was dead,
Or safely put in bed on the rocky road to Dublin.

Chorus

The boys in Liverpool, when in the dock I landed,
Called myself a fool, I could no longer stand it,
My blood began to boil, my temper I was losin'.
And poor old Erin's Isle they all began abusin'
'Hurrah! my boys', says I, my shillelagh I let fly,
Some Galway boys were by, they saw I was a
hobblin'.
Then, with a loud hurray! they joined me in the fray,
And then we cleared the way for the rocky road
to Dublin.

The Rose of Tralee

William P Mulchinock

*It's cringe-inducing, tacky and utterly
tasteless. The contest, that is, not the song.
That's pretty good. There go my free passes
for this year's show. Darn!*

The pale moon was rising above the green moun-
tain,
The sun was declining beneath the blue sea;
When I strayed with my love to the pure
crystal fountain,
That stands in the beautiful vale of Tralee.

Chorus:

She was lovely and fair as the rose of the summer,
Yet 'twas not her beauty alone that won me.
Oh no, 'twas the truth in her eyes ever dawning,
That made me love Mary, the Rose of Tralee.

The cool shades of evening their mantle
were spreading,
And Mary, all smiling, sat listening to me;
The moon through the valley her pale rays was
shedding,
When I won the heart of the Rose of Tralee.

Chorus

On the far fields of India, mid war's bloody thunder,
Her voice was a solace and comfort to me;
But the cold hand of death has now torn us asunder,
I'm lonely tonight for my Rose of Tralee.

Chorus

IF I WIN I WOULD LIKE TO DEDICATE
MY TIME TO HELPING LITTLE
CHILDREN AND SAVING THE WHALES

Spancil Hill

Michael Considine

Another chap yearning for his lost homeland and his lost love. There are so many of these it's a wonder there's anyone left in the bleeding country at all. At all, at all, at all, at all.

Last night as I lay dreaming of pleasant days gone by,
My mind being bent on rambling to Ireland I did fly.
I stepped on board a vision and sailed out with the wind,
Till I gladly came to anchor at the cross of Spancil Hill.

It being the twenty third of June, the day before the fair,
Sure Ireland's sons and daughters, they all assembled there.
The young, the old, the brave and the bold, their duties to fulfil,
There were jovial conversations at the fair of Spancil Hill.

I called to see my neighbours, to hear what they might say,
The old were getting feeble and the young ones turning grey.
I met with tailor Quigley, he's as brave as ever still,
Sure he always made my breeches when I lived in Spancil Hill.

I paid a flying visit to my first and only love,
She's as pure as any lily, and as gentle as a dove.
She threw her arms around me, saying 'Johnny I love you still',
She is Mack the Ranger's daughter, the pride of Spancil Hill.

I thought I stooped to kiss her, as I did in days of yore,
Says she, 'Johnny you're only joking, as you often were before.'
The cock crew on the roost again, he crew both loud and shrill,
And I awoke in California, far, far from Spancil Hill.

But when my vision faded, the tears came in my eye,
In hope to see that dear old spot, some day before I die.
May the joyous King of Angels his choicest blessings spill,
On that glorious spot of nature, the cross of Spancil Hill.

The Spanish Lady

Traditional

Ah yes! A song with a bit of everything – an exotic foreign beauty, a man with a foot fetish and a chorus comprised of words from no known dialect on earth. What more could you ask for?

As I went out through Dublin City
At the hour of twelve at night,
Who should I see but a Spanish lady
Washing her feet by candle light.
First she washed them, then she dried them,
Over a fire of amber coals,
In all my life I ne'er did see
A maid so sweet about the soles.

Chorus:

Whack fol the toora loora laddy,
Whack fol the toora loora lay.
Whack fol the toora loora laddy,
Whack fol the toora loora lay.

I stopped to look but the watchman passed,
Says he, 'Young fellow, the night is late,
Along with you home or I will wrestle you
Straight away through the Bridewell gate.'
I threw a look to the Spanish lady,
Hot as the fire of amber coals,
In all my life I ne'er did see
A maid so sweet about the soles.
Chorus

As I walked back through Dublin City
As the dawn of day was o'er,
Who should I see but the Spanish lady
When I was weary and footsore.
She had a heart so filled with loving
And her love she longed to share,
In all my life I ne'er did see
A maid who had so much to spare.

Chorus

I've wandered north and I've wandered south,
By Stoneybatter and Patrick's Close,
Up and around by the Gloucester Diamond
And back by Napper Tandy's house.
Old age has laid her hands on me,
Cold as a fire of ashy coals,
But where is the lonely Spanish lady
Neat and sweet about the soles?

Chorus

As I was leaving Dublin City
On that morning sad of heart,
Lonely was I for the Spanish lady
Now that forever we must part.
But still I always will remember,
All the hours we did enjoy,
But then she left me sad at parting
Gone forever was my joy.

Chorus

Nice feet!

The Waxies' Dargle

Traditional

You just can't argue with a title like that. The Waxies, if you're interested, refers to the candlemakers. And the Dargle is the river which reaches the shore of Ireland near Bray in County Wicklow. The Waxies' Dargle was their annual outing, or piss-up, in more contemporary parlance. Now there's some useless information to bore your friends with the next time you're in the pub.

Says my oul' wan to your oul' wan
Will ye come to the Waxies' Dargle?
Says your oul' wan to my oul' wan,
Sure I haven't got a farthing.
I've just been down to Monto town
To see uncle McArdle
But he wouldn't lend me half a crown
To go to the Waxies' Dargle.

Chorus:

What are ye having, will ye have a pint?
Yes, I'll have a pint with you, sir,
And if one of us doesn't order soon
We'll be thrown out of the boozer.

Says my oul' wan to your oul' wan
Will ye come to the Galway races?
Says your oul' wan to my oul' wan,
With the price of my oul' lad's braces.
I went down to Capel Street
To the pawn shop moneylenders,
But they wouldn't give me a couple of bob
On my oul' lad's red suspenders.

Chorus

Says my oul' wan to your oul' wan
We have no beef or mutton',
But if we go down to Monto town
We might get a drink for nothin'.
Here's a piece of good advice
I got from an oul' fishmonger:
When food is scarce and you see the hearse
You'll know you've died of hunger.

Chorus

Whiskey In The Jar

Traditional

For anybody under forty who is contemplating singing this at a hooley, a word of warning: when it was originally written, there was no such thing as an electric air guitar solo.

As I was going over the Cork and Kerry mountains
I met with Captain Farrell and his money he was counting.
I first produced my pistol and then produced my rapier,
Saying, 'Stand and deliver, for you are a bold deceiver'.

Chorus:

Musha ring dumma do dumma da,
Whack for my daddy-o,
Whack for my daddy-o,
There's whiskey in the jar.

I counted out his money, and it made a pretty penny.
I put it in my pocket and I brought it home to Jenny.
She sighed and she swore that she never would deceive me,
But the devil take the women, for they never can be easy.

Chorus

I went into my chamber all for to take a slumber,
I dreamt of gold and jewels and for sure it was no wonder.

But Jenny took my charges and she filled them up with water,
And sent for Captain Farrell to be ready for the slaughter.

Chorus

'Twas early in the morning before I rose to travel,
up comes a band of foot men and likewise Captain Farrell.
I first produced my pistol, for she stole away my rapier,
But I couldn't shoot the water so a prisoner I was taken.

Chorus

If anyone can aid me, it's my brother in the army,
If I can find his station in Cork or in Killarney.
And if he'll come and save me, we'll go roving near Kilkenny,
And I swear he'll treat me better than my own dear darling Jenny.

Chorus

Now some men take delight in the carriages a-rolling,
And others take delight in the hurling and the bowling.
But I take delight in the juice of the barley,
And courting pretty fair maids in the morning bright and early.

Wild Colonial Boy

Traditional

We sent the Aussies the wild colonial boy to pillage and plunder their warm and fair land. They sent us 'Neighbours' in revenge. The bastards!

There was a wild colonial boy, Jack Duggan
was his name,
He was born and raised in Ireland, in a place
called Castlemaine;
He was his father's only son, his mother's
pride and joy,
And dearly did his parents love the wild colonial
boy.

At the early age of sixteen years he left his
native home,
And to Australia's sunny shore he was inclined
to roam;
He robbed the rich, he helped the poor, he shot
James MacEvoy,
A terror to Australia was the wild colonial boy.

One morning on the prairie, as Jack he rode along,
A-listening to the mocking bird, a-singing a
cheerful song;
Up stepped a band of troopers: Kelly, Davis
and Fitzroy,
They all set out to capture him, the wild colonial boy.

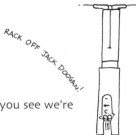

RACK OFF JACK DOOGAN!

Surrender now, Jack Duggan, for you see we're
three to one,
Surrender in the King's high name, you are a
plundering son;
Jack drew two pistols from his belt, he proudly
waved them high,
'I'll fight, but not surrender,' said the wild colonial
boy.

He fired a shot at Kelly, which brought him
to the ground,
And turning round to Davis, he received a
fatal wound;
A bullet pierced his proud young heart, from
the pistol of Fitzroy,
And that was how they captured him, the
wild colonial boy.

The Wild Rover

Traditional

The most popular Irish party-piece in the history of Irish party pieces, it's a cautionary tale of a man filled with guilt for a wild life spent consuming vast quantities of whiskey and beer, usually sung by some gobshite who's just consumed vast quantities of whiskey and beer.

I've been a wild rover for many's the year,
And I've spent all my money on whiskey and beer,
But now I'm returning with gold in great store,
And I never will play the wild rover no more.

Chorus:

And it's no, nay, never,
No, nay, never no more,
Will I play the wild rover,
No, never no more.

I went into an alehouse I used to frequent,
And I told the landlady my money was spent.
I asked her for credit, she answered me 'nay,
Such custom as yours I could have any day'.

Chorus

I took from my pockets ten sovereigns bright,
And the landlady's eyes opened wide with delight.
She says 'I have whiskey and wines of the best,
And the words that I spoke sure were only in jest'.

Chorus

I'll go home to my parents, confess what I've done,
And I'll ask them to pardon their prodigal son.
And when they've caressed me as oft times before,
I never will play the wild rover no more.

Chorus

Colin Murphy hasn't got two notes in his head. He has a singing voice that has been recorded and used to torture people in Central American prisons. A doctor in the Eye and Ear hospital once used his voice to help dislodge a stubborn piece of ear wax in an elderly patient. Unfortunately, it also dislodged the patient's pacemaker. If you encounter him at a hooley, leap to your feet, this book in hand, and make sure you sing before he does. Your very sanity may depend on it.

Seven generations of Donal O'Dea's clan have been musical geniuses. And then came Donal, whose early attempts to play the accordion ultimately resulted in Ireland's first noise pollution legislation. He is the only person in the State who is actually banned from coming within thirty metres of a music shop. He has compiled this book of songs 'just to spite the lot of them'. Next year he embarks on his first One Man Band World Tour. Be afraid. Be very afraid.